Learn **French** with

Max et Mathilde

Les Couleurs – Colours

A catalogue record for this book is available from the British Library

Published by Ladybird Books Ltd
80 Strand, London, WC2R ORL
A Penguin Company

2 4 6 8 10 9 7 5 3 1

Image credits:
page 9: © Dorling Kindersley, page 13: Brian Cosgrove © Dorling Kindersley

ISBN: 978-140930-187-5

Printed in China

Je m'appelle:

My name is:

. . . .

A few tips for grown-ups!

The most practical and enjoyable way to learn French with
Max et Mathilde is to listen to the CD and read along, listening
carefully to the pronunciation and then repeating the phrases.

Listen to the CD more than once. Repetition and singing along
will reinforce the vocabulary and phrases in the book.

Let the pictures guide your child. A translation appears at the back of the
book rather than on the page itself to avoid word-for-word translation.

On the right-hand page, the dialogue delivered by Max et Mathilde
is just as French children would speak to each other.

The most important thing is to maintain your child's enthusiasm, motivation
and interest in learning French. Above all, keep it simple and fun!

"Bonjour"

Tu vas apprendre tes couleurs.
Tu vas t'amuser!

"Je m'appelle Max."

"Je m'appelle Mathilde."

Le chien
s'appelle Noisette.

rouge

Les ballons sont rouges.

un

deux

trois

quatre

cinq

1

2

3

4

5

Il y a cinq ballons.

jaune

Les fleurs sont jaunes.

vert

L'arbre est vert.

"Nous jouons
dans le jardin."

noir

Le parapluie est noir.

orange

Les carottes sont orange.

rose

La glace est rose.

bleu

Le ciel est bleu.

"Regarde le bateau, Max!"

Translation and questions

"Bonjour!" "Hello!"

Tu vas apprendre tes couleurs. You're going to learn your colours.

Tu vas t'amuser! You'll have fun!

"*Je m'appelle Max.*" "My name is Max."

"*Je m'appelle Mathilde.*" "My name is Mathilde."

Le chien s'appelle Noisette. The dog's name is Noisette.

Rouge Red

Les ballons sont rouges. The balloons are red.

"*Un, deux, trois, quatre, cinq.*" "One, two, three, four, five."

"*Il y a cinq ballons.*" "There are five balloons."

Ask your child how many balloons there are: "**Combien de ballons y a t-il?**"

Jaune Yellow

Les fleurs sont jaunes. The flowers are yellow.

"*Regarde-moi!*" "Look at me!"

Ask your child to find the yellow butterfly: "**Trouve le papillon jaune!**"

Vert Green

L'arbre est vert. The tree is green.

"*Nous jouons dans le jardin.*" "We're playing in the garden."

Ask if your child likes playing in the garden: "**Aimes-tu jouer dans le jardin?**"

Noir Black

Le parapluie est noir. The umbrella is black.

"Il pleut." "It is raining."

"Nous sommes tristes." "We are sad."

Ask what the weather is like: "Quel temps fait-il?"

page 12-13

Orange Orange

Les carottes sont orange. The carrots are orange.

"J'adore manger des carottes!" "I love eating carrots!"

"Moi, je déteste les carottes!" "I hate eating carrots!"

Ask what colour the carrots are: "De quelle couleur sont les carottes?"

page 14-15

Rose Pink

La glace est rose. The ice cream is pink.

"Je mange une glace à la fraise." "I am eating a strawberry ice cream."

"Je bois de la limonade." "I am drinking lemonade."

Ask if your child likes ice cream: "Aimes-tu la glace?"

page 16-17

Bleu Blue

Le ciel est bleu. The sky is blue.

"Regarde le bateau, Max!" "Look at the boat, Max!"

Ask what colour the boat is: "De quelle couleur est le bateau?"

page 18-19

Now let's play a game!

Can you remember all your colours?
Find out by answering the questions below.
You can also test your friends, or even your parents!

De quelle couleur...?
What colour is...?

De quelle couleur sont les ballons?
What colour are the balloons?

Les ballons sont...

De quelle couleur sont les fleurs?
What colour are the flowers?

Les fleurs sont...

De quelle couleur est l'arbre?
What colour is the tree?

L'arbre est...

De quelle couleur est le parapluie?
What colour is the umbrella?

Le parapluie est...

De quelle couleur sont les carottes?
What colour are the carrots?

Les carottes sont...

De quelle couleur est la glace?
What colour is the ice cream?

La glace est...

De quelle couleur est le bateau?
What colour is the boat?

Le bateau est...

Now listen to Max et Mathilde on the CD as they take you through the colours. Chant out loud and sing along with them!

Les Couleurs

Rouge et jaune,
Vert et noir,
Toute les couleurs
Nous allons voir!
Orange et rose,
Le ciel est bleu.
Regarde avec nous
Les jolies couleurs!

The Colours

Red and yellow, green and black, we're going to see all the colours!
Orange and pink, the sky is blue. Look at the pretty colours with us!

"À bientôt!"